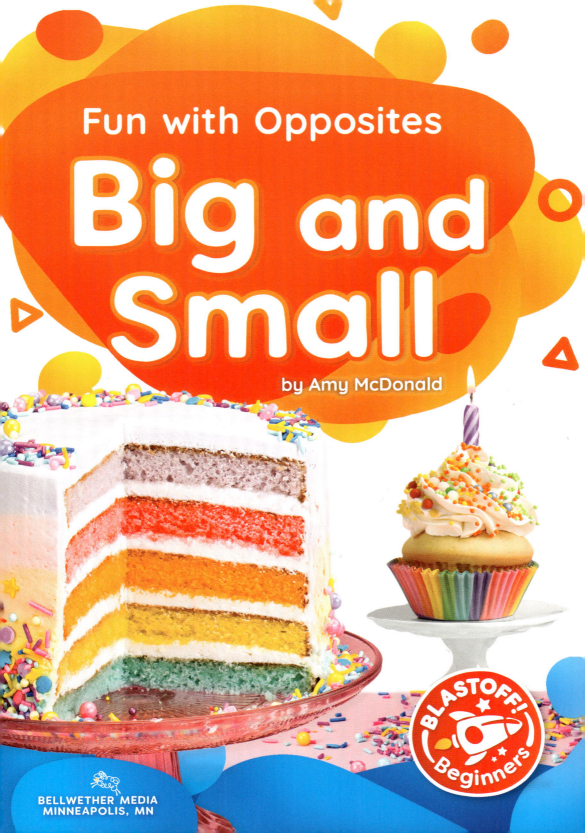

Blastoff! Beginners are developed by literacy experts and educators to meet the needs of early readers. These engaging informational texts support young children as they begin reading about their world. Through simple language and high frequency words paired with crisp, colorful photos, Blastoff! Beginners launch young readers into the universe of independent reading.

Sight Words in This Book

a	big	her	more	up
and	can	I	one	we
are	each	is	the	
at	get	it	they	
be	have	look	this	

This edition first published in 2026 by Bellwether Media, Inc.

No part of this publication may be reproduced in whole or in part without written permission of the publisher. For information regarding permission, write to Bellwether Media, Inc., Attention: Permissions Department, 3500 American Blvd W, Suite 150, Bloomington, MN 55431.

Library of Congress Cataloging-in-Publication Data

LC record for Big and Small available at: https://lccn.loc.gov/2025003227

Text copyright © 2026 by Bellwether Media, Inc. BLASTOFF! BEGINNERS and associated logos are trademarks and/or registered trademarks of Bellwether Media, Inc. Bellwether Media is a division of FlutterBee Education Group.

Editor: Rebecca Sabelko   Designer: Laura Sowers

Printed in the United States of America, North Mankato, MN.

Table of Contents

My Toy	4
Two Opposites	6
Big and Small Things	12
Big and Small Facts	22
Glossary	23
To Learn More	24
Index	24

My Toy

Mom drives
a big truck.
I have a small one.

Two Opposites

Big and small are sizes.

Big things take up more room. They can be heavy.

Small things take up less room.

Big and Small Things

A sunflower is big.
Its seeds are small.

seeds

A **boulder** is big.
A **pebble** is small.

pebbles

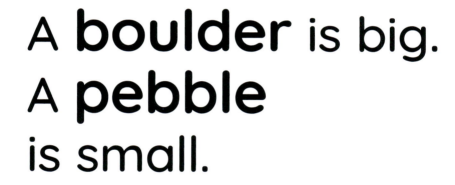

The dog is big. Her puppies are small.

This cake is big.
We each get
a small piece.

Look at this toy.
Is it big or small?

Big and Small Facts

Big and Small Around Us

big swing

small toys

big slide

Something Big and Small

dog

puppy

Glossary

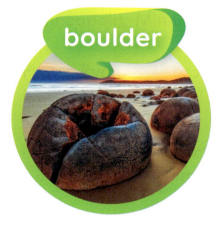

boulder

a big rock that is hard to move

pebble

a small rock that fits in your hand

To Learn More

ON THE WEB

FACTSURFER

Factsurfer.com gives you a safe, fun way to find more information.

1. Go to www.factsurfer.com.

2. Enter "big and small" into the search box and click 🔍.

3. Select your book cover to see a list of related content.

Index

boulder, 14, 15
cake, 18, 19
dog, 16, 17
heavy, 8
mom, 4
pebble, 14

piece, 18, 19
puppies, 16, 17
room, 8, 10
seeds, 12
sizes, 6
sunflower, 12

toy, 20
truck, 4

The images in this book are reproduced through the courtesy of: JFunk, front cover; New Africa, front cover; Artush, p. 3; Anasta_Rass, p. 4; Anna Pasichnyk, pp. 4-5; LightField Studios, pp. 6-7; Juice Flair, pp. 8-9; angellodeco, pp. 10-11; shablovskyistock, p. 12; Andreas von Mallinckrodt, pp. 12-13; xpixel, p. 14; Gary C. Tognoni, pp. 14-15; Eric Isselee, p. 16; Rita_Kochmarjova, pp. 16-17; Lia Koltyrina, pp. 18-19; Krakenimages.com, pp. 20-21; Tanakorn.kr, p. 22 (top); Anna Averianove, p. 22 (dog); Nick Chase 68, p. 22 (puppy); Greg Brave, p. 23 (boulder); WrightAdventurePhotos, p. 23 (pebble).